Finding meaning in a text

Two men walked into the rainforest. Moments before, the forest had been alive with the sounds of squawking birds and howling monkeys. Now all was quiet as the creatures watched the two men and wondered why they had come.

The larger man stopped and pointed to a great Kapok tree. Then he left.

The smaller man took the axe he carried and struck the trunk of the tree.

By Lynne Cherry

1 How many men walked into the forest?

_____

2 What sounds could have been heard in the forest before the men arrived?

_____

3 Why do you think the animals all went quiet?

_____

_____

4 How do you think the animals feel about what is going on?

_____

_____

5 Write down two ideas about what you think might happen next.

_____

_____

Character portraits

1 Collect your ideas for a character portrait by writing descriptions around the picture.

Name _____

Age _____

Personality

_____

_____

_____

_____

_____

_____

Likes _____

_____

_____

Dislikes _____

_____

_____

2 Describe what they look like.

_____

_____

3 Write what others say about them.

_____

_____

Exploring dialogue

1 Put speech marks into these sentences to show where the direct speech is.

a   Hello stranger, where have you been all day said Mum.

b   Has anyone forgotten their lunch asked the
    teacher.

2 Look for these words for **said** in the word search:

> asked   told   answered   pleaded   begged   shouted
> bellowed   whispered   mumbled   replied   barked
> complained   giggled   cried   whined   grumbled   spoke
> called   hissed   gasped   sang   joked   huffed   teased

a	s	k	e	d	a	c	e	s	j	o	t	o	l	d
n	w	h	i	n	e	d	k	h	o	m	e	g	f	d
s	p	u	o	p	a	l	u	o	k	d	t	i	s	e
w	n	f	d	e	b	i	n	u	e	g	e	g	r	j
e	e	f	a	r	b	a	m	t	d	e	s	g	c	l
r	x	e	p	l	e	a	d	e	d	e	r	l	o	s
e	e	d	m	e	g	n	t	d	o	n	e	e	b	w
d	u	s	a	n	g	r	e	p	l	i	e	d	i	h
d	g	a	s	p	e	d	m	e	r	e	d	g	n	i
m	c	r	i	e	d	e	u	t	e	a	s	e	d	s
i	l	y	j	g	r	u	m	b	l	e	d	a	n	p
c	a	l	l	e	d	i	b	n	g	s	p	o	k	e
b	u	d	c	o	m	p	l	a	i	n	e	d	e	r
r	a	a	h	i	s	s	e	d	k	t	h	n	l	e
b	e	l	l	o	w	e	d	e	b	a	r	k	e	d

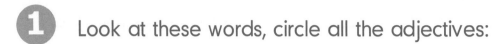

Using adjectives

1 Look at these words, circle all the adjectives:

table	purple	mountain	skiing	leather
banana	spotted	drink	enormous	dinner
tortoise	speedy	delicious	shark	slippery

2 Re-write these sentences by adding adjectives to describe the nouns.

a   The children ate cakes.

_____

_____

b   The family sat together to watch the football final on television

_____

_____

3 Write as many adjectives as you can to describe the following:

a   A book you have enjoyed.

_____

b   Your favourite food.

_____

c   The weather today.

_____

Powerful verbs

Powerful verbs give more detail about an action.

1 Look at the powerful verbs in the cloud below. Write each verb in the correct column of the table.

whispered   wandered   noticed   glimpsed   plodded
stared   hiked   argued   examined   strolled   laughed
pranced   replied   cackled   recognised   spotted
bounced   gazed   shouted   explained   paced

walked	looked	said

2 Now add one word of your own to each column.

Improving descriptions

1 Look at the picture. Write a sentence describing:

a Something you can see.

_____

_____

_____

b The weather.

_____

_____

c What you can hear.

_____

_____

2 Now re-write your sentences choosing the best words you can to explain and describe.

a _____

_____

b _____

_____

c _____

_____

Self-assessment

Unit I

Let's look at themes in stories

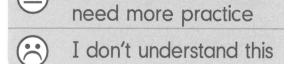

	😊 I understand this well
😐	I understand this but need more practice
😞	I don't understand this

Learning Objectives	😊	😐	😞
Reading			
I can answer questions about a story.			
I can understand a text from clues given by the author.			
I can identify different types of stories and story themes.			
Writing			
I can use powerful verbs and adjectives to make my writing better.			
I can explore words used for starting and finishing speech.			
I can use punctuation to show dialogue.			
I can write a detailed description of a setting.			
I can write details about characters.			
Speaking and listening			
I can join in with discussions and respond to what others say.			
I can listen to other people and make sensible comments.			

I need more help with ...

_____

_____

_____

_____

_____

 **Exploring non-fiction**

Alphabetical order

1 Re-write these authors and illustrators names in alphabetical order by their surname:

> Michael **Rosen**   Axel **Scheffler**   Jackie **French**
> Jacqueline **Wilson** Debjani **Chatterjee** Anthony **Horowitz**
> Valerie **Bloom** Michael **Morpurgo** Sue **Hendra** Tove **Jansson**

_____   _____

_____   _____

_____   _____

_____   _____

_____

2 Give another example where you have seen alphabetical order used. _____

3 Write the titles of two fiction and two non-fiction books you have read.

Fiction:

_____

_____

Non-fiction:

_____

_____

A contents page

Tigers of the world

Contents

1 What does a Contents page do? Tick the correct answer. It:

    a   gives you a list of all the chapters/sections in the book and which pages they are on ☐

    b   helps you to find something in alphabetical order. ☐

2 Circle the features you would expect to find in Chapter 2.

maps   photographs/pictures of tigers
bullet points   sub-headings   few or no pictures
information about what tigers eat

3 Which chapter would help you understand what tigers eat? _____

4 Each chapter has a title and a question. Write a question in the space for Chapter 4.

5 Which page would you turn to if you wanted to find out what endangered species meant? _____

6 How do you use an index? _____

_____

Compound words

1 Circle the compound words:

activity   newspaper
breakfast   cycling   window
octopus   headline   children

2 Choose a word from each cloud to create a compound word:

book   tea   some
back   sun   any

thing   pack   one
mark   shine   pot

a _____

b _____

c _____

d _____

e _____

f _____

3 Choose one compound word and write a sentence with it in.

_____

4 Explain why the word **children** is **not** a compound word.

_____

Comprehension

1 The glossary descriptions from a book about sharks are muddled up! Read them carefully then draw a line to match up the words with the descriptions. The first one has been done for you.

marine life	a baby shark
dorsal fin	when sharks get over-excited when they are hungry, sometimes biting each other
pup	openings at the sides of a shark's body where water enters its body
endangered species	something that lives in the sea or ocean
feeding frenzy	side fins usually found under the gills
gills	the fin that sits on the shark's back
pectoral fins	when the last creature of a species dies and there will be no more
extinct	an animal at risk of being wiped out of existence because there are so few of them

2 Use the glossary above to write two sentences of your own about sharks.

_____

_____

Fact and fiction

1 Read these sentences and decide if they are a fact or an opinion. Write **fact** or **opinion** next to each sentence.

a   Summer is the best season. _____

b   Paris is the capital city of France. _____

c   The Sumatran Tiger is an endangered species. _____

d   Ice cream is so delicious. _____

2 Finish these sentences and write fact or opinion next to them:

a   Everyone should go and see _____

b   _____ always sings beautifully.

c   A _____ is a large wild cat.

d   The tickets cost _____

3 Write in the spaces below:

a   Two facts

_____

_____

b   Two opinions

_____

_____

4 Write sentences explaining facts and opinions:

A fact is _____

An opinion is _____

Instructions

1 Choose *bossy* verbs from the bowl to add to this recipe:

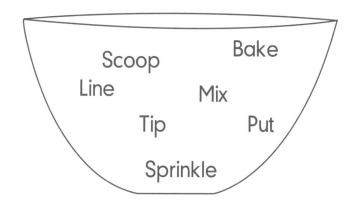

_____ a baking tray with baking parchment.

_____ the butter and sugar into a large bowl
and cream together.

_____ in the flour.

_____ together until it has all stuck together.

_____ the mixture out on to a floured surface
and knead to a soft dough then press into the baking tray.

_____ the shortbread in an oven on a medium
heat for about **20** minutes.

_____ with sugar and leave to cool on a wire rack.

2 What title could this recipe have?

_____

3 What features could be added to these instructions to make them
more eye-catching?

_____

_____

Presenting information

1 Choose the correct word from the box and write it in the space to complete the sentence:

> table
> title
> pictures
> caption
> sub-heading
> bullet points

a _____ separate information with a dot or numbers.

b A _____ is written under a picture or photograph.

c _____ add visual details to the written descriptions.

d A _____ gives information in columns.

e The _____ gives the first clues about what a text is about.

f A _____ is a type of heading used to separate information.

2 Where might you see the features above? What types of text might have these features?

_____

_____

_____

3 Pick one of your answers to question 2 and list which of the features from the box above you would expect to find in it.

_____

_____

Self-assessment

Unit 2

Exploring non-fiction

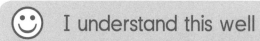

		I understand this well
:)		
:|		I understand this but need more practice
:(		I don't understand this

Learning Objectives	:)	:|	:(
Reading			
I can work out the meaning of unknown words by reading around them.			
I can understand and use the terms *fact, fiction* and *non-fiction.*			
I can use contents and index pages in non-fiction books to find information.			
I can identify different ways that information is shown on a page.			
Writing			
I can organise words in alphabetical order.			
I can use and spell compound words.			
I can use a dictionary to find the spelling and meaning of words.			
I can identify nouns, verbs and adjectives.			
I can record information in a table.			
I can write my own non-fiction text.			
Speaking and listening			
I can give clear instructions.			
I can listen and remember instructions.			

I need more help with …

_____

_____

_____

_____

_____

Poetry fun!

Unit 3

Reading poetry

Off to the sweet shores of Africa,
Off, with my harp and harmonica,
I'll follow the walking, talking drum
To the land, where the sunbirds hum.

Off to the sweet shores of Africa,
To fields of palm and paprika,
I'll watch the kingly eagle fly
Beneath the clear blue sky.

Off to the sweet shores of Africa,
Off, in my jar of tapioca,
I'll ride on the River Nile's rolling crest
Till my jar comes to rest.

Uzo Unobagha

1 Practise reading the poem aloud a few times using the commas to pause and the full stops to breathe.

2 Practise changing your voice for the two different characters.

Glossary

tapioca: hard white grains from the cassava plant, used to make puddings.

Synonyms

1 Write three other words that mean the same as the following words:

a   small

b   walked

c   talking

_____   _____   _____

_____   _____   _____

_____   _____   _____

2 Re-write these sentences replacing the underlined words with a synonym:

a   My <u>Dad</u> has a <u>fast</u> boat.

_____

b   The kitten took a <u>rest</u> on the <u>sofa</u>.

_____

c   They <u>loved</u> eating the <u>delicious</u> cookies.

_____

3 Spot the odd one out in this list of synonyms for 'good' and draw a circle around it:

fine   kind   polite   hungry   generous   well-mannered

Nouns, verbs and adjectives

① Fill in the missing nouns, verbs and adjectives in the crossword clues below.

> red   gobbled   drinking   playground
> enormous   climbed   bicycle

1. Ishaq _____ out of bed.

2. Somebody has _____ up all the cake!

3. The shoes didn't fit me, they were _____.

4. My _____ has orange reflectors on the pedals.

5. The stop sign has a _____ light.

② Write clues for the two words that are left.

6 _____

7 _____

③ Fill in the crossword.

Shape poem

1 Read the shape poem.

Oliver the Octopus
Underneath the sea
Swimming very slowly
Looking for his tea
Makes a little bubble
Gives a little grin
"Hi there, fishes!
Come on in ..."

By Tony Mitton

2 Write synonyms for the words below.

slowly   _____   looking   _____

little   _____   grin   _____

3 Now add your synonyms into the poem.

Oliver the Octopus

Underneath the sea

Swimming very _____

_____ for his tea

Makes a _____ bubble

Gives a little _____

"Hi there, fishes!

Come on in ..."

21

Writing and performing

1 Create strings of rhyming words.

    a   peeling   feeling   wheeling   squealing

    b   trying   frying   _____   _____

    c   funny   _____   _____   _____

    d   sit   _____   _____   _____

2 Pick one string of rhyming words above and add nouns to create a simple rhyming poem, for example:

Sammy's peeling,

Sontash's feeling,

Sonny's wheeling,

Joshua's squealing!

_____

_____

_____

_____

3 Read and perform your poem to someone.

Self-assessment

Unit 3
Poetry fun!

😊	I understand this well
😐	I understand this but need more practice
🙁	I don't understand this

Learning Objectives	😊	😐	🙁
Reading			
I can use punctuation to help me read with expression.			
I can understand why authors choose particular words in poems.			
I can answer questions about a poem.			
I can infer meanings that are not written on the page.			
I can read a range of poems and identify the main idea of each poem.			
Writing			
I can find synonyms for everyday words.			
I can find examples of nouns, verbs and adjectives.			
I can write a poem, thinking about words that rhyme.			
Speaking and listening			
I can read aloud using expression.			
I can practise to improve my performance when reading aloud.			

I need more help with ...

_____

_____

_____

_____

Unit 4 Let's study an author

Reading fiction

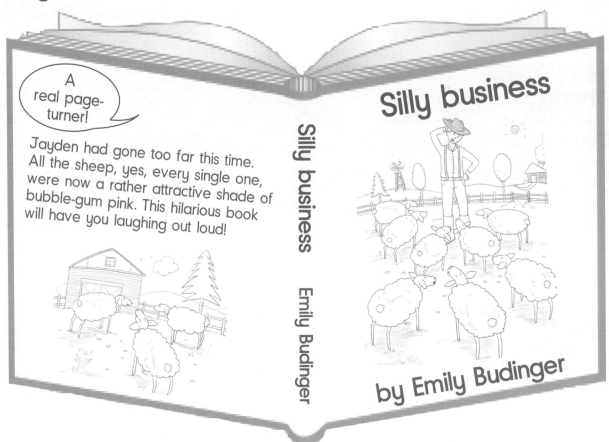

A real page-turner!

Jayden had gone too far this time. All the sheep, yes, every single one, were now a rather attractive shade of bubble-gum pink. This hilarious book will have you laughing out loud!

Silly business

Silly business

Emily Budinger

Silly business

by Emily Budinger

1 Look at the title of this book. What clues about the story does it give us?

_____

2 What clues does the blurb tell us about the character Jayden?

_____

3 What question comes into your head about this book?

_____

4 Look at the speech bubble on the back cover. What does it mean?

_____

Homonyms

1 Find the homonyms below in the word search.

l	o	n	g	e	b	u	c
m	y	i	l	t	i	e	h
a	i	b	a	r	k	d	i
b	o	w	s	l	l	n	p
l	e	x	s	a	i	d	e
j	a	m	e	p	e	e	p
g	e	n	s	t	a	l	k
m	a	r	c	h	e	m	v

glasses
chip
stalk
jam
bark
march
bow
lie
tie
long

2 Now write each of the homonyms next to the correct meaning below.

a   Part of a plant, or to follow someone. _____

b   The noise a dog makes, or the outside of a tree. _____

c   Third month, or a way of walking. _____

d   Opposite of short, or to really want something. _____

e   To tell an untruth, or what you do when you lounge on the sofa. _____

f   Used to shoot an arrow, or to tie a ribbon. _____

g   Two people win a race, or worn in a special knot under a shirt collar. _____

h   Sticky sweet food, or too much traffic. _____

i   To pour drinks into, or to help you see better. _____

j   A small piece of glass, or a French fry. _____

25

Sentence variety

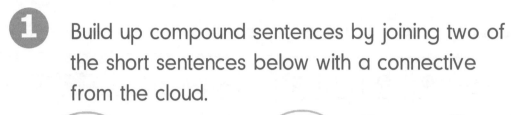

1 Build up compound sentences by joining two of the short sentences below with a connective from the cloud.

> but   so that   before   if   until   when   although
> however   even though   because   and so

They played the best I have ever seen.   My mum called me in.
It was raining hard.   My dinner was ready.
My team did not win.   We hurried to the bus stop.

a _____

b _____

c _____

2 Re-write the sentence and change the connective so the sentence makes sense:

a I like to eat my dinner (until) I go dancing.

_____

b He was very calm (so that) his sister was the total opposite.

_____

c We have to make our beds (even though) we can go out.

_____

3 Choose any connective and create a compound sentence of your own.

_____

Looking at pronouns

1 Finish these sentences by choosing a pronoun from the cloud below.

> I   you   he   she   we   my   me
> they   them   him   her   it

a   _____ is always late.

b   _____ only ever wants to play football.

c   How do _____ always win?

2 Swap the underlined word or words with a pronoun and re-write the sentences:

a   Did <u>Kara and Seren</u> make it to the beach?

_____

b   <u>Isabella</u> always gets up early.

_____

c   <u>Jose and Gene</u> played with the kitten then fed <u>the kitten</u>.

_____

d   If <u>Rodrigo</u> tidies his room then <u>Rodrigo's</u> mother will let <u>Rodrigo</u> go out to play.

_____

_____

3 Write a sentence about your family using pronouns.
Try to include one of these: we, they, them.

_____

Setting descriptions

1 Look at the setting and write words or phrases to describe what you can:

a   See _____

_____

b   Hear _____

_____

c   Smell _____

_____

2 Use your notes about the picture and ideas from the word bank to write a setting description.

> **Word bank**
>
> island   boats   harbour
> bay   fishermen   sunshine

_____

_____

_____

_____

Impact words

1 Look at these simple verbs then write a powerful verb.
The first one has been done for you.

a shout *exclaim*

b eat _____

c took_____

d jump _____

2 Pick two powerful verbs and illustrate them in the boxes below.

 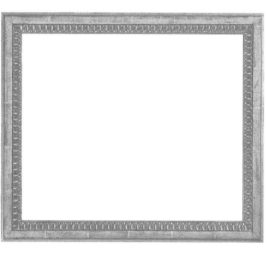

_____ _____

3 Write one sentence for each powerful verb you have chosen that will interest and excite the reader. Use the ideas in the word bank to help you.

a _____

_____

b _____

_____

Word bank

rich treasures   colourful   amazing sunset

sweet smelling   rocky mountains   dangerous

murky river   rickety bridge

Describing a character

 1 These words could all be used to describe a character.

> grumpy   caring   lazy   untidy   playful   brave
> bad   rude   selfish   cruel   gentle   unhappy
> kind   wimpy   fun   beautiful   jolly

Write down three more words that could be used to describe a character.

_____   _____   _____

 2 a Pick three words that might be used to describe a good character:

_____   _____   _____

b Use those three words to write a sentence about the character.

_____

_____

 3 a Now pick three words that might be used to describe a bad character:

_____   _____   _____

b Use those three words to write a sentence about the character.

_____

_____

Self-assessment

Unit 4
Let's study an author

	I understand this well
	I understand this but need more practice
☹	I don't understand this

Learning Objectives	☺	☺	☹
Reading			
I can infer meaning from other words in a sentence.			
I can answer questions about a story.			
I can talk about characters in different books by the same author.			
I can identify words that are used to describe characters.			
Writing			
I can identify words that are homonyms.			
I can use a dictionary to find the meaning of words.			
I can use simple, compound and complex sentences.			
I can identify pronouns in a sentence.			
I can write a book review to say what I think about a book.			
I can write a character portrait.			
I can plan main points to help me write stories.			
I can organise my writing into sections or paragraphs.			
Speaking and listening			
I can use drama to move like a character in a story.			

I need more help with ...

_____

_____

_____

_____

Unit 5 — Which text type?

Spelling rules

Remind yourself of these spelling rules.

> For most verbs you can add –**ing**, –**ed** or –**s** to the root word.
>
> For example:
> show = show**ing**

> For most verbs, if the verb ends in an **e**, you drop the **e** and then add –**ing**, or –**ed** to the root word.
>
> For example:
> come = com**ing**

> For most verbs, if the verb ends in **ie**, you change **ie** to **y** and add –**ing** to the root word.
>
> For example:
> tie = t**y**ing
>
> BUT not when adding –**ed** or –**s** = ti**ed**, tie**s**

1 Choose the right spelling rule and re-write the words below with the –**ing**, -**ed** and –**s** endings. The first one has been done for you.

		-ing	-ed	-s
a	smile	smiling	smiled	smiles
b	cry			
c	joke			
d	cook			
e	walk			
f	play			
g	cover			

Layout of instructions

1 Read the text and label the layout features in this recipe:

numbered bullet points   sub-heading   title

How to make French bread pizza

You will need:
A chunk of French bread stick
Tomato sauce
Grated cheese

1.   First wash your hands and put on an apron.

2.   Cut the bread in half along its longest side.

3.   Spread the tomato sauce along the flat side.

4.   Sprinkle cheese on top.

5.   Place on a baking tray and cook in a medium
     oven for 5–10 minutes or until the cheese has melted.

6.   Serve by cutting into slices.

Additional toppings can be added, such as mushrooms,
onions or peppers.

2 Use colour and illustrations to make the recipe more
attractive to the reader.

Prefixes and suffixes

1 Use the prefixes and suffixes to generate new words:

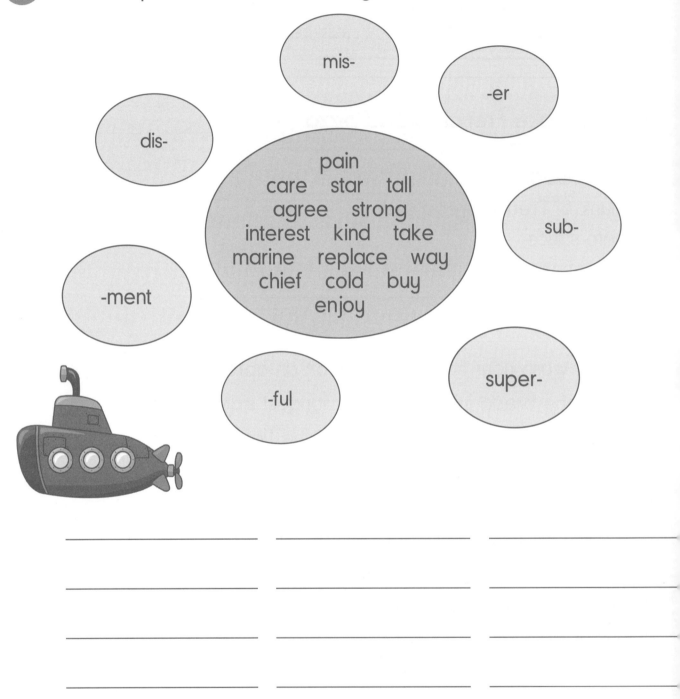

_____   _____   _____

_____   _____   _____

_____   _____   _____

_____   _____   _____

2 Circle the prefix or suffix in each of these words:

a tallest **b** unhappy **c** preschool **d** mistrust **e** agreement

Crossword

1 Work out the missing words from the clues and fill in the crossword puzzle.

> dictionary   newspaper   biography   atlas   explanation

I. _____ texts explain and tell us about something.

2. A _____ is a book written about a real person.

3. An _____ contains maps and information about different countries.

4. A _____ is written in alphabetical order and explains what words mean.

5. A _____ has news reports about events that have happened.

Understanding tenses

 1 **a** Draw a line to match the sentence with the correct tense.

| past | present | future |

I am eating my lunch.

I will leave school early tomorrow.

We all sang well yesterday.

b Underline the verbs in each sentence above.

2 Write the present and future forms of each verb:

a Yesterday I danced.   I am _____   I will _____

b Yesterday I juggled.   I am _____   I will _____

c Yesterday I swam.   I am _____   I will _____

3 **a** Write a sentence about something you did yesterday. (Past)

_____

b Write a sentence about what you are doing now. (Present)

_____

c Write a sentence about something you will do next. (Future)

_____

Comprehension

My trip up the Sky Tower

Last year, my brother and I flew by aeroplane to the city of Auckland. New Zealand is made up of two main islands and Auckland is the biggest city on the north island.

As soon as we arrived we noticed what a beautiful city it was, with its huge harbour and bay full of sailing boats. Our first stop was the impressive Sky Tower. It is **328** metres tall and we were going up it!

After buying our tickets we stepped into a glass-fronted lift which would take us to the viewing platform. It was a smooth ride up but I felt a bit giddy. Then we stepped out and were amazed by the stunning views across the whole city. Eventually we had to return to the ground. My brother and I said it was the longest but best ride in a lift ever!

1 Underline the time connectives in the extract.

2 Who did the writer travel with? _____

3 Where is the Sky Tower? _____

4 Write down two words from the text used to describe Auckland.

_____

5 What is the purpose of the text? _____

6 Pick out words or phrases that tell you the author enjoyed his trip. _____

_____

More than one

1 Complete the captions below.

one _____   three _____

2 Fill in the spaces to complete the singular and plural table:

Singular	Plural
cat	
apple	
	keys
	parties
shoe	
	boxes
lunch	
	dishes
strawberry	
donkey	

3 Write another example of singular and plural.

One _____ and many _____

4 Underline the nouns and write S (Singular) P (Plural) next to each sentence.
a   Two rabbits hid.   _____
b   The snake slept peacefully.   _____
c   She dropped the plate.   _____

5 Choose a pair of nouns and write a sentence for each:

baby/babies   fox/foxes   blueberry/blueberries

_____

Self-assessment

Unit 5
Which text type?

 I understand this well

 I understand this but need more practice

 I don't understand this

Learning Objectives			
Reading			
I can improve my understanding of prefixes and suffixes.			
I can read and follow instructions.			
I can notice ways that information is set out on a page.			
I can identify the main purpose of a text.			
I can find information in non-fiction texts to answer questions.			
I can identify layout and style features in different texts.			
Writing			
I can learn the rules for adding **–ing**, **–ed**, **–s** to verbs.			
I can improve the way that I use tenses.			
I can understand the terms 'singular' and 'plural'.			
I can write a first-person account.			
Speaking and listening			
I can listen to and remember a set of instructions.			
I can take part in discussion, responding to what other people say.			

 I need more help with ...

_____

_____

_____

_____

_____

6 Unit **Acting fun!**

How do you feel?

1 Look at these children. Write how you think they are feeling at the top of each picture.

a _____   b _____   c _____

_____   _____   _____

_____   _____   _____

2 Think about how each of the children above might move, behave and speak. Use the words below to help you and add your own exciting verbs and adjectives around each picture.

> ## **Word bank**
>
> excitedly   nervously   slowly
> shrieking   loudly   slouching   carefully
> hurriedly   stumbling   quickly

3 Write something one of the children might say and remember to say *how* they say it. For example: "Yippee! I am the winner!" he shrieked excitedly.

_____

Words for meaning

1 Look at these actions:

> waving hand   rounded shoulders   jumping about   smiling
> crying   head down   clapping hands   biting nails
> skipping   frowning   looking worried   whispering
> hand covering face   eyes looking down   looking happy

Choose the best words from the box above to describe these children.

a _____

_____

_____

b _____

_____

_____

2 Look at these emotions:

> angry amazed upset happy excited
> embarrassed sad shy elated overjoyed relaxed
> worried fed up miserable sulky

Write down in the table below which emotions you think would be shown by the actions. The first one has been done for you.

Actions	Emotions
clapping hands	happy, excited
frowning	
hands covering face	
crying	
eyes and mouth wide open	
finger pointing	
red face	
eyes looking down, arms crossed	

Reading a playscript

Tiddalick the Thirsty Frog
Scene I Outback Australia

(Tiddalick sits in the middle of the stage. The other animals graze quietly in the background.)

Reader I: In times long ago, when the deserts were covered in green grass and the rivers were full and flowing ...

Reader 2: There lived a large frog called Tiddalick.

Reader 3: He was the largest of all the frogs.

Reader 4: The biggest and fattest frog ever.

Reader 5: So very big, that next to him the tallest trees looked like twigs and the highest mountains looked like small hills.

Reader I: When Tiddalick croaked ... the mountains shook and the animals trembled in fear.

Reader 2: Now, being such a big frog, Tiddalick was very thirsty.

Reader 3: One morning, Tiddalick went to the river to have a drink.

(Tiddalick hops forward.)

Reader 4: He drank so much that the river ran dry.

Reader 5: But the greedy frog was still thirsty.

By Mark Carthew

1 Read the play extract in a group of six. Take it in turns to read the different parts and to be Tiddalick.

2 Act out the scene in your group.

3 Together decide what you think happens next. Add a new scene to your play.

Playscripts

1 Write down two differences between a playscript and a story.

_____

_____

2 Which do you prefer? Please explain your answer.

_____

_____

3 Think about the playscripts you have looked at. Write true or false next to each of these statements.

a   The names of the characters are written down the left side next to what they say. _____

b   Playscripts use sub-headings and bullet points. _____

c   Stage directions tell the actors what to do when they are saying their lines. _____

d   The setting for each scene is described at the end of the book.

_____

e   Speech marks are used to show the spoken parts. _____

f   The spoken parts always have lines that rhyme. _____

4 Using the words in the box organise the text to look like a playscript:

> We never get to do the things I want!
> Wesley: (Stamping his foot)

_____

_____

Stage directions

1 Read these speech bubbles:

> Who's there?

> I don't understand, what has happened to all the cookies?

> That was your last chance. Just go!

> I'm not sure if I can write, my hands are so cold.

2 Now re-write them below with the appropriate stage direction:

a (Shouting and wagging a finger.) _____

_____

b (Shivering, rubbing hands together.) _____

_____

c (Scratching his head and looking puzzled.) _____

_____

d (Creeping slowly into the room.) _____

_____

3 Write stage directions to go with these lines. Remember to use brackets:

a _____

It's half past ten!

b _____

I don't feel very well.

c _____

I can't find my shoes!

Self-assessment

Unit 6
Acting fun!

		I understand this well
		I understand this but need more practice
	😦	I don't understand this

Learning Objectives	🙂	😐	😦
Reading			
I can understand how words are chosen to show how a character feels.			
I can use stage directions to read a playscript with expression.			
I can answer questions about a playscript.			
I can read and talk about books by the same author.			
Writing			
I can use different words for *said*.			
I can use the correct punctuation in a playscript.			
I can read my own writing to check for spelling, grammar and punctuation.			
I can write playscripts based on my reading.			
Speaking and listening			
I can practise reading aloud to improve my performance.			
I can act out the part of a character in drama.			
I can read playscripts using different voices.			

I need more help with ...

_____

_____

_____

_____

Communicate with me

Comprehension

 Read the text and answer the questions below.

Helvetica ▾ 12 ▾ ■ B I U ≡ ≡ ≡ ≣▾ ➡▾	

To:	Malita
Cc:	
Subject:	Visit
From:	Seb ▾
≡ ▾	**Signature:** None ▾

Hi Malita, best cousin in the world!

I've got great news! Granny is now much better and has told me she wants to visit you, but even better she said I could come with her. YAY!!! I'm so excited about our trip. We will be arriving next Thursday and staying for ten days. At the moment I'm trying to decide what to pack as I'm only allowed to bring one case. ☹ We will have to take two buses, then a train, then another bus and one more train. We're leaving home early but it will take most of the day to get there so expect us by 6 p.m. Email me back soon and tell me what we'll be doing so I can pack the right stuff!

Bye for now,

Your favourite cousin, Seb! ☺

a Who wrote this and why did they write it? _____

_____

b How will Seb and Granny travel? _____

_____

c How many suitcases will Seb bring? _____

d Where do you think this text has come from? Circle one
   answer.   A letter?   An email?   A postcard?

e What clues from the text helped you answer question d?

_____

_____

Verbs

1 Sort these verbs into present and past tense.

> held   go   draw   creep   grew   dived
> came   drink   kept   learn

Present	Past
_____	_____
_____	_____
_____	_____
_____	_____
_____	_____

2 Look at this table and fill in the missing verbs.

Present form of verb	Simple past form of verb	Past participle of verb
break	broke	broken
see	saw	seen
take	took	taken
	gave	

3 Choose a word from each column and use it in a sentence.

a _____

b _____

c _____

Adding suffixes to verbs

1 Think about the spelling rules you have learnt and add the suffixes –**ing**, –**ed** and –**s** to these verbs:

		–ing	–ed	–s
a	hope	_____	_____	_____
b	dance	_____	_____	_____
c	rub	_____	_____	_____
d	model	_____	_____	_____

2 Choose the correct root word to fill in the spaces. Change the spellings of the words if you need to.

> hop   snap   end   stop

a   Last part of a story: _ _ _ ing.

b   The car _ _ _ _ _ _ ed just in time.

c   Jumping on one foot: _ _ _ _ _ ing.

d   I _ _ _ _ _ _ ed the twig with my foot.

3 Pick a root word and a suffix to fill in the spaces.

> skip   hop   look   talk   –ed –ing

a   Yesterday I was _____ to my neighbour.

b   Mariyah will be _____ with her new rope.

c   The rabbit _____ quickly away from danger.

d   Where have you _____ for your football boots?

Pronouns

 Sort these pronouns by drawing a line to the correct heading. Watch out as some will go to both headings!

(Pronouns for people and animals)   (Pronouns for things or objects)

he
me
us
they
him
it
we
I
you
she
them
her

2 Re-write these sentences swapping the underlined words for a pronoun:

a   The table was wobbling; one of <u>the table's</u> legs was loose.

_____

b   Khin loved <u>Khin's</u> cat.

_____

c   Mari told everyone about <u>Mari's</u> new baby brother.

_____

d   When the children arrived at the swimming pool <u>the children</u> were so excited.

_____

_____

e   The bus was early, which was strange because <u>the bus</u> was usually late.

_____

_____

Compound words

1 Find these compound words in the wordsearch.

> sleepover   woodshed   crossword
> dishwasher   weekend   greenhouse
> strawberries   inside   cannot
> sandpaper   hailstorm   forget   spaceship
> goldfish   tightrope

s	a	e	n	e	s	c	r	o	s	s	w	o	r	d
t	l	x	a	s	l	a	f	o	r	g	e	t	c	i
r	h	g	r	e	e	n	h	o	u	s	e	t	i	s
a	a	o	d	t	e	n	l	e	m	p	k	e	n	h
w	i	l	e	i	p	o	d	i	e	a	e	a	u	w
b	l	d	r	g	o	t	e	e	r	c	n	d	n	a
e	s	f	b	h	v	g	n	i	b	e	d	i	n	s
r	t	i	u	t	e	w	o	o	d	s	h	e	d	h
r	o	s	d	r	r	u	m	l	y	h	j	n	g	e
i	r	h	j	o	e	b	i	n	s	i	d	e	a	r
e	m	m	a	p	n	s	a	n	d	p	a	p	e	r
s	w	y	r	e	w	r	i	f	e	r	e	r	o	s

2 Choose two compound words and write them in a sentence.

a _____

b _____

Apostrophes for omission

> she would I they he should
> could is where you do can
> we did who that it

> will am are not
> is had have

1 Join words from each cloud by using an apostrophe for omission. You can use some words more than once. An example has been done for you.

she'll	_____	_____
_____	_____	_____
_____	_____	_____
_____	_____	_____
_____	_____	_____

2 Re-write these sentences changing the underlined words for the longer words. The first one has been done for you.

a   I'm enjoying running, it's such a sunny day!
    I am enjoying running, it is such a sunny day!

b   It was so hot we couldn't move.

   _____

c   My little sister can't tell the time.

   _____

d   Your team played well but didn't win.

   _____

e   You're the best player on our team.

   _____

Pronouns and verbs

1 Choose the correct verb to fill in the space.

> fly   roars   meow   flies   meows   roar

a   What does a dragon do?   It _____.
They _____.

b   What does an aeroplane do?   It _____.
They _____.

c   What does a cat do?   It _____.
They _____.

2 Choose the correct verb and write it in the space.

a   She _____ to have her own computer.
want/wants

b   _____ he have any experience of riding horses?
do/does

c   They _____ not happy about all the mess.
was/were

3 Choose one of the pronouns below and write it in the space.

> he   him   I   them   she   they   her   me

a   _____ scored a goal in the last minute.

b   We gave _____ our tickets.

c   The lunch box got left behind so _____ was hungry.

Purpose for writing

 Read the text and answer the questions.

Hello everyone at home!

Having a brilliant time. Sandboarding lessons are going well and I'm getting better at it every day, but I have lots of bruises! The food has been great. Off on a mountain safety course now so got to go.

Love to all the family,

Maliki

AUSTRALIA
70c
Tasmanian Blue Gum

Mum and Dad

MacDonalds Cottage

16 Hooper Street

Townsville

Brisbane

Australia

a   What type of communication is this?

b   Why was it written?

c   Who is the audience for the writing?

d   What sort of information would you expect to find in this kind of communication?

e   What does Maliki think about the food?

Tenses

1 Underline the verb and re-write the sentences changing them from future to past tense.

a   I will be going shopping with my friends.

_____

b   I will really enjoy playing football with my brothers.

_____

c   Nacho and Dana will eat their lunch together.

_____

d   Darcey will enjoy school today.

_____

2 Write two sentences about something you did last week.

_____

_____

3 Write two sentences about what you will be doing next week.

_____

_____

4 The tenses are muddled in these sentences, re-write them so they make sense.

a   Yesterday I running all the way home.

_____

b   Tomorrow I played with my friends.

_____

Self-assessment

Unit 7
Communicate with me

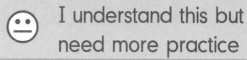

	☺	😐	☹
☺ I understand this well			
😐 I understand this but need more practice			
☹ I don't understand this			

Learning Objectives	☺	😐	☹
Reading			
I can identify the main point of a text.			
I can find meanings beyond what is written in a text.			
Writing			
I can use more powerful verbs.			
I can learn the rules for adding –**ing**, –**ed**, –**s** to verbs.			
I can use and spell compound words.			
I know irregular forms of common verbs.			
I can identify pronouns.			
I can recognise when an apostrophe is used for omission.			
I know that pronouns and verbs have to agree.			
I can write letters.			
I can vary my sentence openings.			
I can use a wider range of sentence types.			
I can decide *who* I am writing to and *why* I am writing.			
Speaking and listening			
I can read aloud with expression.			

I need more help with ...

_____

_____

_____

_____

Unit 8 Traditional stories

Adverbs

1 Choose an adverb from the bubble to describe the verb in these sentences. Re-write the sentence. An example has been done for you.

> quickly
> gently slowly
> greedily
> hurriedly

a   I walked down the road.
   I walked <u>quickly</u> down the road.

b   She ate all the pizza.

   _____

c   I put down the glass.

   _____

d   He climbed the hill.

   _____

2 Write an adverb to answer these questions. Use the Word bank to help you.

a   How did the kangaroo hop? _____

b   How did the moon shine? _____

c   How did she stomp off? _____

d   How did he paint the house? _____

e   How did he tidy up? _____

f   How did the children play? _____

Word bank

badly quickly happily noisily sadly gently
cheerfully neatly carefully brightly angrily

Characters

1 Read the extract and underline words that describe Gracie's character.

Gracie was a fun-loving adventurous girl. She was popular at school with her teachers and with the other children. I guess you could describe her as 'Miss Average'. She wasn't the fastest runner nor was she the slowest. She wasn't top of the class but she certainly wasn't bottom either. She was generous and kind, and she loved animals, especially Mr Marmalade her grey pony.

Everything was good in Gracie's life until the day everything changed …

2 What does the description 'Miss Average' mean?

_____

3 Look at the words you underlined and write down four words to describe a character who has a personality the <u>opposite</u> of Gracie's.

_____   _____

_____   _____

4 Which of these settings would you expect to find in this story? Tick the boxes.

a classroom ☐   a stable ☐   an alien space ship ☐   countryside ☐

5 Write down one idea about what might happen next.

_____

_____

Words for 'said'

1 Look at each picture and the words the people are saying. Choose a word from the Word bank below to write in a word for 'said' in the spaces.

a "Be quiet!" _____ the teacher.

b "I want my Mummy," _____ the toddler.

c "Lets go outside I don't want to wake him up." _____ the baby's mother.

d "What's for dinner? Is it nearly ready? We're starving!" _____ the children.

e "I'm boiling, It's too hot outside!" _____ Raj to his brother.

Word bank

bellowed   whispered   pleaded   asked   blubbered
chattered   begged   grumbled   argued   shouted
cried   wailed   pleaded   moaned   sobbed

Speech marks

1 Turn these speech bubbles into dialogue with speech marks.

a _____

b _____

_____

c _____

d _____

_____

Nouns, verbs and adjectives

1 Match the word and meaning:

An action or doing word.

The name of something.

Describes a noun.

noun

verb

adjective

2 Write these words under the correct heading in the table below.

> stinky   letter   gobbled   purple   eat
> chair   delicious   jump   bicycle   tree
> telescope   sweet   writing   spotty
> hop   cupcake   kind   run

Nouns	Verbs	Adjectives

3 Write one sentence using a word from each box.

_____

Settings in stories

1 Look at this setting. Fill in the table with words and phrases that could describe this setting.

I see...	
I smell...	
I hear...	
I taste...	
I touch...	

2 Use the words and phrases you have written in the table and write two interesting sentences to describe the setting.

_____

_____

_____

Impact words

1 Impact words help create a picture in our minds. Look at these two sentences about Thor:

    a Thor was very angry, he hit his hammer on the ground and it made a loud noise.

    b Thor was now filled with rage, it poured out with each blow of his hammer. The noise he made with it was an incredible roar.

Which sentence has the greatest impact? _____
Underline the words that best create the impact.

2 Write impact words to replace the following words. The first one has been done for you.

    a nice   caring

    b good   _____

    c nasty   _____

    d nice taste   _____

    e bad taste   _____

3 Read the following sentence about a firework going off.

There was a loud bang and then bright lights.

Re-write the sentence by using some of these impact words to create a picture in the reader's mind.

> explosive bang   thunderous bang   colourful sparks flying
> cascading sparkles   a sea of sparkling lights

_____

_____

Paragraphs

1 Paragraphs are a collection of sentences about something and they help us organise our writing.

a   Saj is an eight-year-old boy. He has written two paragraphs to describe:
- the food and drink he likes and dislikes
- his hobbies and interests.

b   Draw a line to show which sentence should go in which paragraph.

Foods and drink Saj likes and dislikes	I like eating lentil curry and naan bread. I look after my pet hamsters – Cosmo and Dinky. I collect miniature cars. I don't like coffee. I love playing football with my friends. I play computer games. I am allowed to watch TV for an hour when my homework is finished. Strawberry is my favourite flavoured milkshake. I have never and I never will eat spinach! I like listening to music. I like to drink mango lassi. I hate bananas when they are too soft. _____ _____	Saj's hobbies and interests

2 Add one more sentence for each heading above.

3 Write a paragraph about the food and drink you like or dislike.

_____

_____

Self-assessment

Unit 8
Traditional stories

	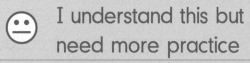 I understand this well
	I understand this but need more practice
	I don't understand this

Learning Objectives	😊	😐	☹
Reading			
I can identify words that make an impact on a text.			
I can understand hidden meaning in a text.			
Writing			
I can identify vocabulary for introducing speech.			
I can use adverbials to show links between events.			
I can use prefixes and suffixes.			
I can collect examples of nouns, verbs and adjectives.			
I can use my reading to help me write dialogue.			
I can write character portraits.			
I can develop my descriptions of settings in stories.			
I can plan the main points of a story.			
I can organise my writing into sections and paragraphs.			
Speaking and listening			
I can take turns to talk about my character portrait with a partner.			

_____

_____

_____   I need more help with ...

_____

Unit 9 Perform it!

Plurals

1 Think about the spelling rules for plurals. Circle the correct spelling for these plurals.

a   ladyes   ladies
b   bananas   bananes

c   dresss   dresses
d   paintes   paints

e   computeries   computers
f   strawberries   strawberryes

g   lolles   lollies
h   brushies   brushes

2 Join the singular noun to the plural noun below. The first one has been done for you.

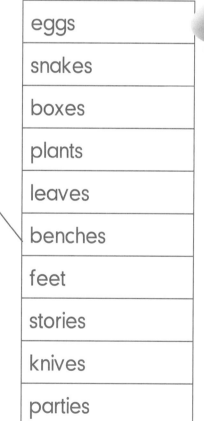

bench	eggs
foot	snakes
story	boxes
leaf	plants
knife	leaves
snake	benches
party	feet
plant	stories
egg	knives
box	parties

Rhyming words

 Poets often use rhyming words to create impact.
Sort these words into sets of rhyming words.

> more   ball   feet   treat   bet   late   tall   let   poor   win
> seat   ring   net   sing   door   set   hate   get   tore   thing
> beat   fate   heat   hall   mate   fall   rate   call   floor   king

2 Write down one more set of rhyming words, starting with 'log'.

Writing poetry

1 Use the Word bank or your own ideas to fill in the spaces in this poem.

> **Word bank**
>
> twisting   copying   skipping   skating   jumping   jogging
> tapping   crossing   sewing   driving   resting
> dancing   leaping   lounging   sleeping   building

Gerry is crawling

Beau is _____

Lara is _____

Paulo is _____

Heather is _____

Thomas is scooting

Maya is _____

Sol is _____

Dana is _____

Christopher is _____

Kamal is _____

2 Add two more lines to the end of the poem.

_____ is _____

_____ is _____

Writing poetry

1 Look at this acrostic poem for a giraffe:

> **G**igantic long neck
>
> **I**nvisible in tall trees
>
> **R**uns as fast as the wind
>
> **A**frican favourite
>
> **F**luffy tipped tail
>
> **F**our feet called hooves
>
> **E**legant and majestic.

2 Create your own acrostic poem for an elephant:

E _____

L _____

E _____

P _____

H _____

A _____

N _____

T _____

3 Perform your poem to someone.

Performing a poem

Bamboo Tree Frog

Did you know
I change to be
the colour of
my bamboo tree?

On bamboo small
and bamboo large,
I clasp and snooze
in camouflage.

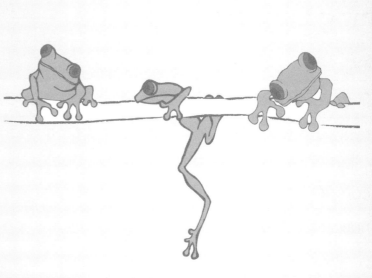

It's mainly greens
and browns I choose
amongst a grove
of slim bamboos.

Red or purple
forestry?
I think that might
bamboozle me!

By Liz Brownlee

Glossary

Bamboozle: to cheat, trick
or confuse someone.

1 Read the poem in your head, noticing the rhythm and the rhyme.
Practise reading it aloud.

2 Perform the poem to someone.

Self-assessment

Unit 9
Perform it!

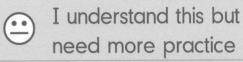

☺ I understand this well

😐 I understand this but
   need more practice

☹ I don't understand this

Learning Objectives	☺	😐	☹
Reading			
I can find words that make an impact in a poem.			
I can read a poem about an iguana and then find more information about iguanas in a non-fiction book.			
I can compare the stucture of two poems.			
I can notice the rhythm and rhyme patterns in a poem.			
I can practise reciting poetry.			
Writing			
I can choose adjectives carefully to make my writing better.			
I can use plurals correctly.			
I can write and perform poems.			
Speaking and listening			
I can read aloud with expression.			
I can change the tone of my voice for different audiences.			
I can improve my performance when reading poems aloud.			

_____

_____

_____

I need more
help with ...

_____

The Publishers would like to thank the following for permission to reproduce copyright material:

Acknowledgements

p3, from *The Great Kapok Tree: A Tale of the Amazon Rainforest* by Lynne Cherry. Copyright © 1990 by Lynne Cherry. Reprinted by permission of Houghton Mifflin Harcourt Publishing Company. All rights reserved; p18, by Uzo Unobagha from *Off to the Sweet Shores of Africa and Other Talking Drum Rhymes*, published by Chronicle Books; p21, *Undersea Tea* by Tony Mitton from *The Works* chosen by Paul Cookson, published by Macmillan Children's Books; p42, *Tiddalick the Thirsty Frog: A play based on an Australian Aboriginal story* retold by Mark Carthew. Reproduced with permission from Mark Carthew © 2007, Pearson Australia, pages 5–7; p68, *Giraffe* by Emily Budinger; p69, *Bamboo Tree Frog* by Liz Brownlee, (*http://www.poetlizbrownlee.co.uk/site/bamboo-tree-frog*).

Although every effort has been made to ensure that website addresses are correct at time of going to press, Hodder Education cannot be held responsible for the content of any website mentioned in this book. It is sometimes possible to find a relocated web page by typing in the address of the home page for a website in the URL window of your browser.

Hachette Livre UK's policy is to use papers that are natural, renewable and recyclable products and made from wood grown in sustainable forests. The logging and manufacturing processes are expected to conform to the environmental regulations of the country of origin.

Orders: please contact Bookpoint Ltd, 130 Milton Park, Abingdon, Oxon OX14 4SB. Telephone: +44 (0)1235 827720. Fax: +44 (0)1235 400454. Lines are open 9.00 a.m.–5.00 p.m., Monday to Saturday, with a 24-hour message answering service. Visit our website at www.hoddereducation.com

© Emily Budinger 2015
First published in 2015 by
Hodder Education,
An Hachette UK Company
Carmelite House
50 Victoria Embankment
London EC4Y 0DZ

Impression number   10
Year   2019 2018

Cover illustration by Sandy Lightley
Illustrations by Marleen Visser
Typeset in Swissforall 14pt
Printed in Great Britain by Hobbs the Printers, Totton, Hampshire

A catalogue record for this title is available from the British Library

ISBN 978 1471 830990

Cambridge Primary

Hodder Cambridge Primary English Stage 3

Hodder Cambridge Primary English is a complete English course supporting the Cambridge Primary English curriculum framework. The books have been written by experienced primary practitioners specifically for Cambridge Primary.

Each unit of work is based on a reading genre within fiction, non-fiction or poetry. The activities cover the objectives from all areas of the Cambridge Primary English curriculum framework: *Reading, Writing* and *Speaking and listening*. The Workbook supports the activities in the Learner's Book and Teacher's Pack.

Each Workbook includes:

- additional activities linked to the Learner's Book, providing further practice to consolidate the objectives

- a learner-friendly self-assessment page at the end of each unit.

The series consists of a Learner's Book, Teacher's Pack and Workbook for each Cambridge Primary stage. Books in the **Hodder Cambridge Primary English** series:

	Learner's Books	Teacher's Packs	Workbooks
Stage 1 (ages 5–6)	9781471831003	9781471831010	9781471831027
Stage 2 (ages 6–7)	9781471830211	9781471830259	9781471830242
Stage 3 (ages 7–8)	9781471830976	9781471830983	9781471830990
Stage 4 (ages 8–9)	9781471830266	9781471830273	9781471830280
Stage 5 (ages 9–10)	9781471830761	9781471830952	9781471830969
Stage 6 (ages 10–11)	9781471830204	9781471830228	9781471830235

For over 25 years we have been trusted by Cambridge schools around the world to provide quality support for teaching and learning. For this reason we have been selected by Cambridge Assessment International Education as an official publisher of endorsed material for their syllabuses.

This resource is endorsed by
Cambridge Assessment International Education

✓ Provides learner support as part of a set of resources for the Cambridge Primary English curriculum framework from 2018

✓ Has passed Cambridge International's rigorous quality-assurance process

✓ Developed by subject experts

✓ For Cambridge schools worldwide

ISBN 978-1-471-83099-0

HODDER EDUCATION

www.hoddereducation.com